P9-BIT-665

a daily
dose of **non**
sense

Published by MQ Publications Limited
12 The Ivories, 6–8 Northampton Street, London N1 2HY
Tel: 020 7359 2244 / Fax: 020 7359 1616
email: mail@mqpublications.com

ISBN: 1-84072-514-1

3 5 7 9 0 8 6 4 2

Printed and bound in Italy

a daily
dose of
non
sense

Cheers !

BY LISA SWERLING & RALPH LAZAR

MQP

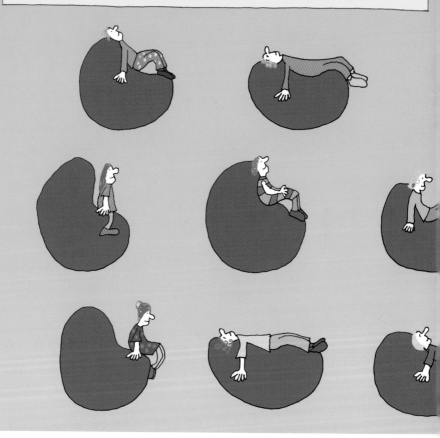

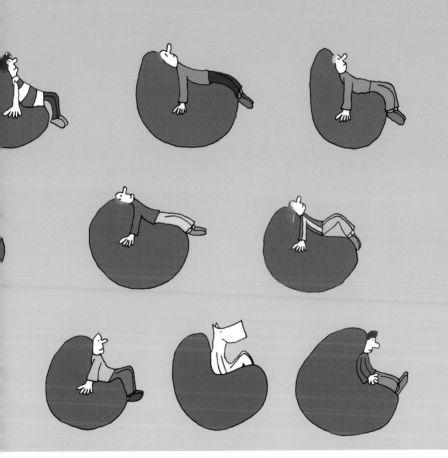

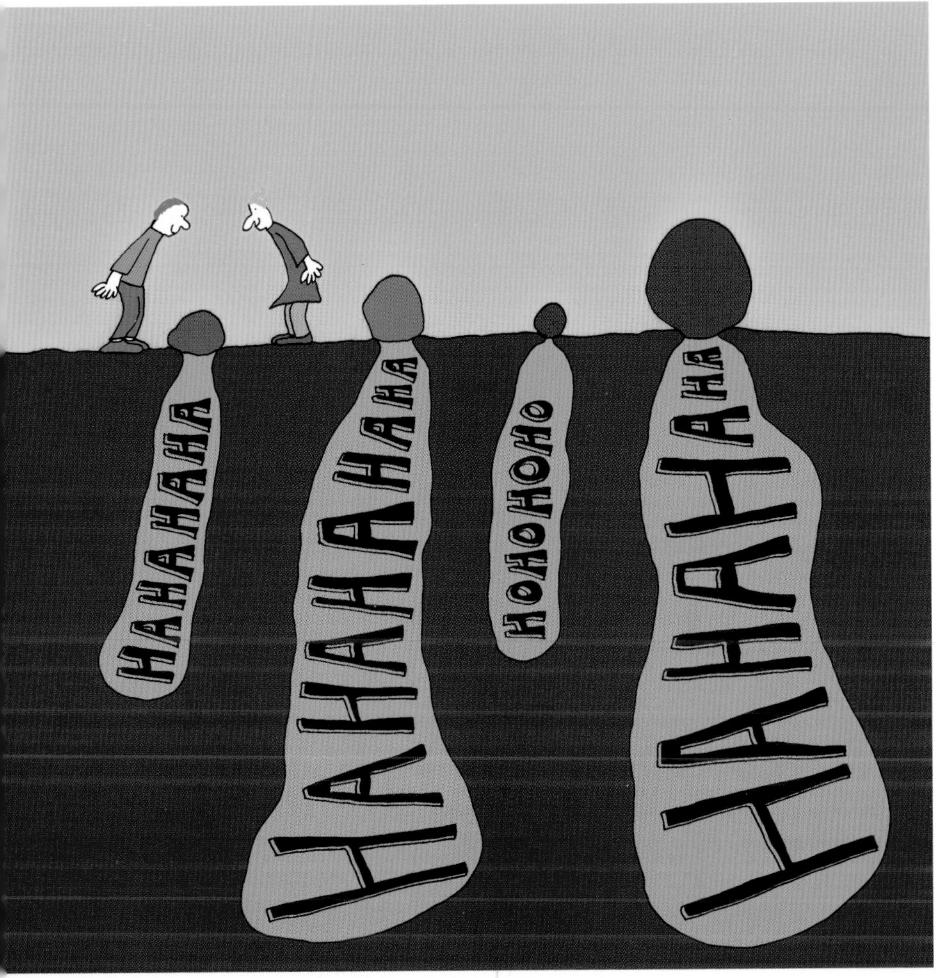
HAHAHAHA
HAHAHAHAHA
HOHOHOHO
HAHAHAHA

hE KNEW THE RELATIONSHIP HAD TO END WHEN HIS ANSWERING-MACHINE BECAME A QUESTIONING-MACHINE

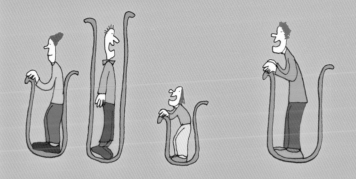

*I*F ANYONE WANTED TO MAKE SMALL TALK, HE'D PULL OUT HIS WIFE EDNA, AND THEY COULD TALK TO HER.

fOUNDER OF THE ALARM CLOCK LIBERATION MOVEMENT

THE WONDER OF NATURE: WHEN ANTS CAME AND CARRIED OFF PETE'S MOTHER-IN-LAW

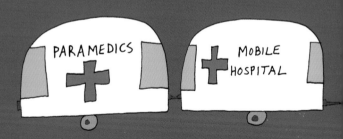

STUMBLING ACROSS THE ANCIENT BRIEFCASE BURIAL GROUNDS

a TOUCH OF BUBBLE BATH MAKES ALL THE DIFFERENCE

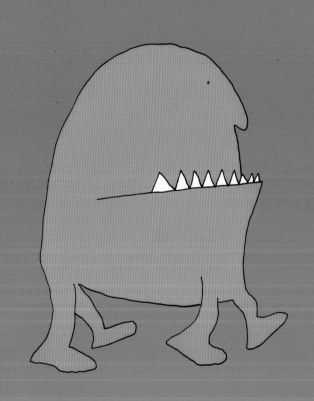

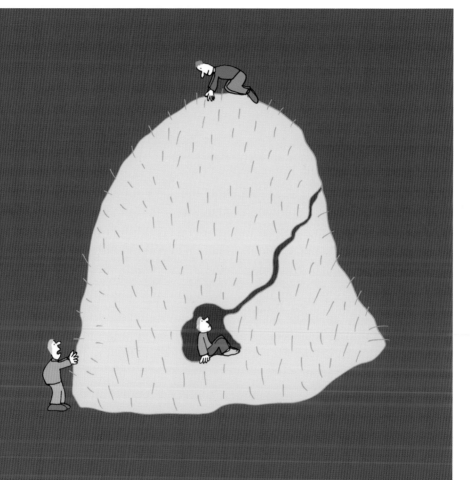

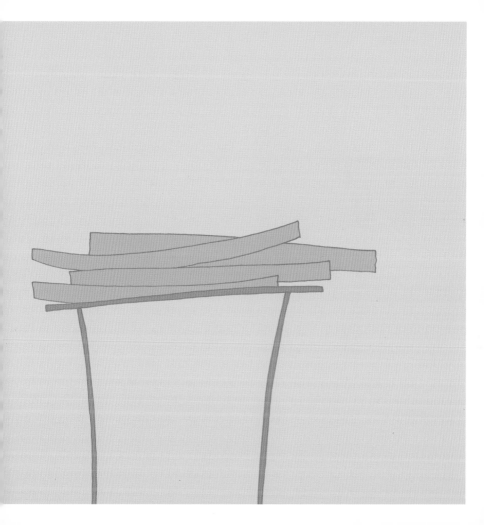

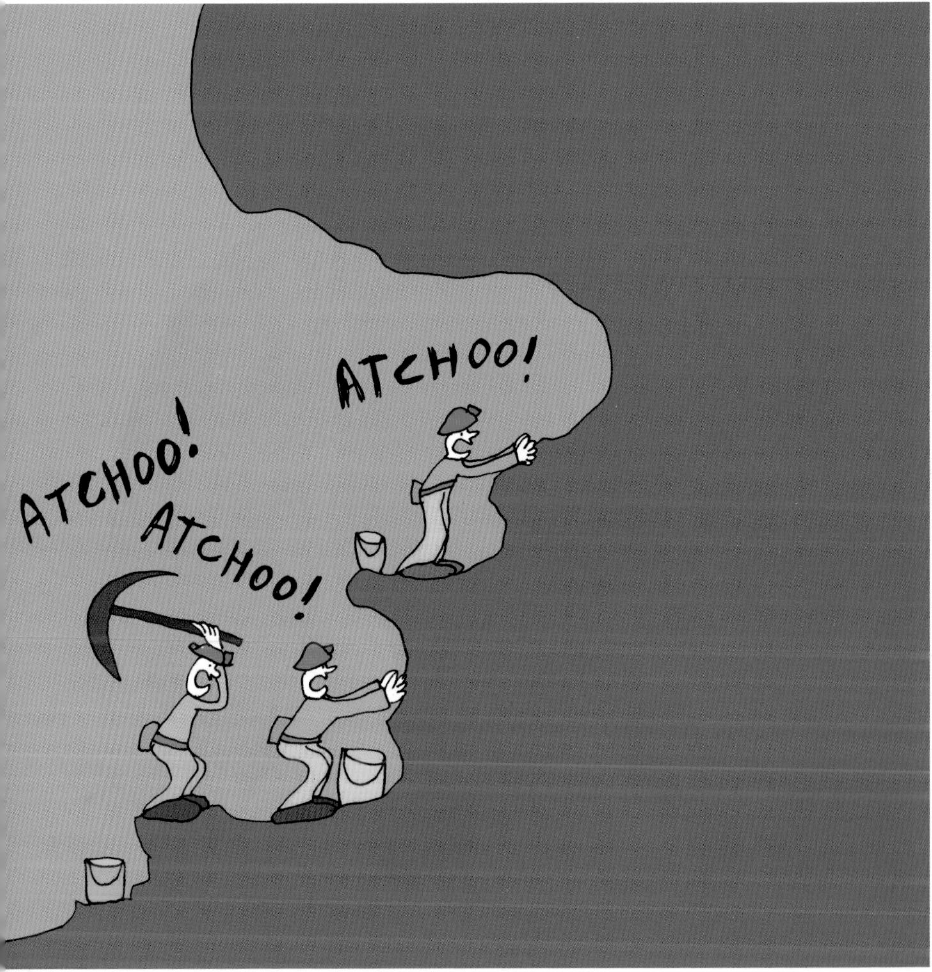
ATCHOO!
ATCHOO!
ATCHOO!

bLESSED WITH THE ABILITY TO SLEEP THROUGH ANYTHING

hE DIDN'T BELIEVE THE SUPERSTITIOUS NONSENSE ABOUT NOT WALKING ON CRACKS IN THE SIDEWALK...

LOVE BETWEEN MAN AND POTPLANT IS INDEED POSSIBLE

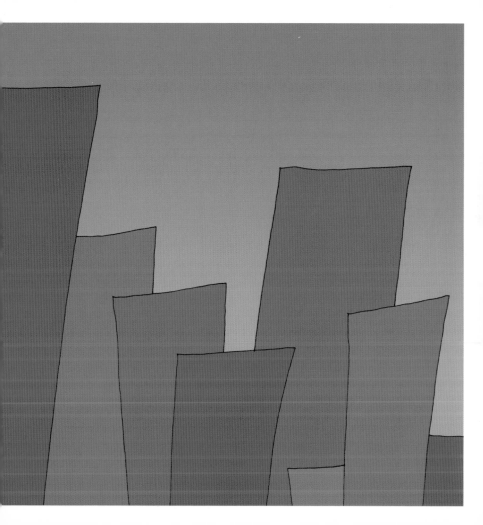

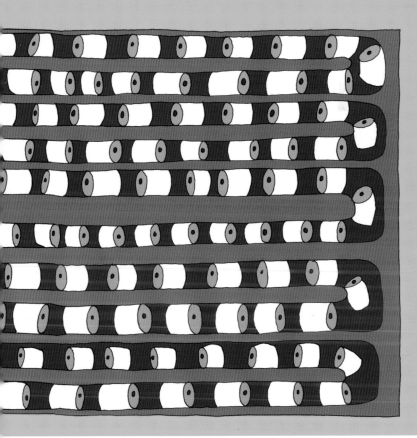

ABOUT THE AUTHORS

Ralph Lazar and Lisa Swerling are currently based in the UK. Their other series include *Harold's Planet* and *Epsilon Osborne, hero of the corporate jungle.*